FEELING
HAPPY
FEELING
SAFE

Michele Elliott
Illustrated by Alice Englander

HODDER AND STOUGHTON
LONDON SYDNEY AUCKLAND

For my grandmother, Katherine, who was kind and loving
For my wonderful children, Charles and James
For all children everywhere, that they may be safe

About the author

Michele Elliott is the leading expert in the UK in teaching children how to protect themselves. She is a child psychologist, teacher and parent. In 1984 she established KIDSCAPE, the national campaign for children's safety, of which she is the Director. The KIDSCAPE Code, which children may also meet in school, is at the end of this book. Michele Elliott has chaired World Health Organisation and Home Office Working Groups on the subject of preventing child abuse. She is the author of *Keeping Safe, a Practical Guide for talking with Children* for adults and *The Willow Street Kids, It's Your Right to Be Safe* for 6-11 year olds. KIDSCAPE has schools programmes for all ages of children.

British Library Cataloguing in Publication Data

Elliott, Michele
    Feeling happy, feeling safe.
    I. Children. Abuse by adults. Prevention
    I. Title   II. Englander, Alice
    362.76

    ISBN 0-340-54664-6 (hbk)
    ISBN 0-340-55386-3 (pbk)

First published 1991
Third impression 1992

Published by Hodder and Stoughton Children's Books, a division of Hodder and Stoughton Ltd, Mill Road, Dunton Green, Sevenoaks, Kent TN13 2YA

Designed by Zena Flax

Printed in Italy by L.E.G.O., Vicenza

Recommended materials

For parents

Keeping Safe, a Practical Guide to Talking with Children Michele Elliott, New English Library. Low-key, practical advice for talking with children about potentially dangerous situations.
How to Help them Stay Safe Michele Elliott. A free guide from KIDSCAPE for parents.

For children under 6

BBC, Cosmo and Dibs 'Keep Safe' video with poster and teaching notes by Michele Elliott. Five short stories on one video dealing with getting lost, touching, secrets, etc. Available from KIDSCAPE.
The Body Book Claire Rayner, Piccolo. Easy-to-understand explanations which help young children learn about their own bodies.
We Can Say No David Pithers and Sarah Green, Beaver. Explains about strangers and tells children not to go off with anyone unless they first tell an adult.

For children under 11

The Willow Street Kids Michele Elliott, André Deutsch/Pan. A lively group of friends deal with a variety of problems such as bullying, stranger danger, flashers and a 'bad' secret. Chosen for the *Good Book Guide* in 1987.

For teenagers

Safe, Strong and Streetwise Helen Benedict, Hodder and Stoughton. A practical book with sound ideas for teenagers about keeping safe.

For schools

KIDSCAPE has teaching programmes for under fives, five to elevens and teenagers.

For deaf children

You Choose The Keep Deaf Children Safe Project, National Deaf Children's Society. A colour picture book with signing, which explains how to keep safe.

Notes for adults

Feeling Happy, Feeling Safe has been specially written for young children. It will help them to understand how to keep safe and whom to tell if they feel unsafe. Reading this book with your children will also help you to talk with them in a low-key, reassuring way about what to do if they are bullied, get lost, are approached by a stranger, or even by a known adult who may try to harm them. We all want to educate children to be alert to danger without depriving them of their innocence, and this is what my book aims to help you do.

If children are taught from the earliest possible time to understand that their safety is important, they will continue to develop their innate sense of self-preservation. It is this self-protection we want to encourage in children. The messages in the book all deal with a child's right to be safe. The stories foster the idea that children's bodies belong to them and give them suggestions for protecting themselves, usually with help from caring adults. It would be unrealistic not to include adult help, but sometimes children need to be taught to ask for help, even from their own parents.

One Mum wrote to me about her three-year-old daughter, who had been abducted while she was in a park with the child. The mother glanced away for a minute, only to look up and see her child being led away by a man. She ran after the abductor, grabbed her daughter back and rang the police. Then she asked her daughter why she hadn't shouted, as Mum was only yards away. Her daughter replied that she started to, but the man said to keep quiet, so she did. Her instinct for survival had been outweighed by her desire to be obedient.

There may also be times when children need to ask for help from a stranger, or a stranger offers help to a lost child. As we teach children never to talk to someone they don't know, this issue must be carefully handled. In the story 'Getting Lost', Anne has to decide whether to ask for help from the lady who works in the shop, though Gran turns up before she does so. Parents can explain to their young children that they may have to break the stranger rule if they are lost and cannot find their Mummy or Daddy or whoever is looking after them. In that case, they may have to accept help from a stranger.

In 'Someone You Don't Know', James has to accept help. But he doesn't get too close or take a stranger's hand. In this case, the strangers ring from a public telephone, so James does not have to go in a house with them. He does go along to the telephone box.

It is a difficult dilemma for parents to decide how much information to give little ones. It may be too confusing for young children to say that sometimes you talk to strangers, sometimes not. You can tell them that the *only* time they should ever talk to, or go with a stranger is if they are lost, and then they should find someone with children. Tell them not to go into anyone's house, but to wait while the person telephones for help. This is what I did with my children, but every parent must decide what is best for their own. Thankfully, most adults are well-meaning and will help a child in difficulty. Sometimes we just have to give children the best advice we can and trust to the good side of human nature.

Whatever you decide with your children, practise what you have agreed. Let them play out a situation and show them where to stand and how to keep their distance. In fact, it's a good idea to practise all the safety ideas in this book.

Children learn best by doing things in a safe environment with supportive adults. Use Mike and Emma, Anne and James to help your child learn that it's all right to make a fuss, to get away, disobey and tell a grown-up if he or she feels unsafe in any way. Children need these messages and reassurances so that they will know what to do in case anything happens. The child who was abducted in the park instinctively knew what to do, but she needed to be told that she was right to do it.

The messages for children are developed gently through the stories. The earlier ones show situations which many children experience, such as getting lost and being bullied. The later ones go on to more difficult problems, such as dealing with strangers and with people who try to persuade children to keep kisses or hugs secret. Each story is short and has its own ending, so you can decide how much to read to your child at any one time.

The following points may help when you're reading the stories:

Feeling Safe
Ask children where they feel safe and whom they feel safe with, to help them think what it means to be safe. To most young children 'safe' means not being scared, feeling happy. One child told me that feeling safe was 'not being in the zoo with snakes'. Well said!

Getting Lost
In one class of 20 children aged five, 13 children said they had been lost at least once and that they had been very frightened. Many adults can vividly remember being lost as children, and often say they had no idea what to do then. It's important that children have some ideas to help them in case they do get lost. After the story, work out simple rules with your children and practise what to do.

Saying No
We spend our lives teaching children to say yes, but there are times when they must say no to be safe. Children need to be given permission to say no and to be told that they can shout no if someone is trying to harm them. Practise games which allow children to say no, such as:

Adult: 'Would you like a mud and rock sandwich for lunch?'
(Choose something your child does not like.)
Child: 'No.'
Adult: 'Come on, you'll like it.'
Child: 'NO, NO!'

Repeat the exercise with something your child does like, but should say no to, such as a stranger offering sweets or a chance to see baby rabbits.

These simple games can help children develop an assertiveness which may prove invaluable one day, even if you think your children are already too assertive! Just make sure they know it's all right to say no to anyone who tries to harm them or lure them away.

However, there may be times when it isn't possible to say no. Children need to know that they can and should say no when they feel something is not right. But they also need to be told that you will never be angry if they can't say no. The main message to get across is that you want to know if *anything* happens and you will love them no matter what.

Bullies
Unfortunately, most children meet bullies sooner or later. Bullying can be devastating and every child needs to know ways of dealing with bullies. Saying no, getting friends to help, and telling are the ways that Mike and his friends cope with an older bully. You can use this story to discuss why children bully, if you feel that your child is old enough to understand. Bullies are usually sad, lonely and unhappy people who take out their problems on others. Sometimes it works to make friends with a bully, to invite him or her over to play under supervision. It's important to make it clear that you do not condone bullying and that you want to know if it's going on. It's not 'telling tales'.

Someone You Don't Know
Children may already know not to talk to strangers, but young children take people out of the category of stranger very quickly. My youngest son decided that the ice-cream man was his friend for life after just one conversation! Children need to understand that strangers are people you don't know well. For young children, one good method of ensuring that they understand about strangers is to make up a list of people who are not strangers. Work out with your children exactly whom they can go with, but remind them that they should never go *anywhere* with anyone, even someone they know well, without first telling you. I say to my children that they must not talk to anyone they don't know unless Mummy or Daddy (or Gran or Grandad) is there, or they have asked me if they may. I know this might mean hurting the feelings of that sweet old gentleman who may just be saying hello, but young children cannot be expected to know the difference between 'good' and 'bad' strangers. You will want to work out your own rules.

How much you say to your child about what strangers could do to children depends upon the maturity and sensitivity of the child. Some parents say that 'bad' strangers can kill children. This is true, but could make children fearful of everyone. In the book I say that some strangers are nice and some are not, and may hurt children. I leave it to you to explain in more detail, if you feel your child is ready for this information. Eventually all children learn this, if only from sad reports in the media. Some parents use these reports to talk to their children. Again, it depends upon the child.

Touching
Children are very touchy, feely little creatures and loving touch is vital for them. They must not be put off touching, but need to learn that it should never be kept secret and that they can say no to touches they don't like. The children in the

story talk about the touches they like and don't like, which gives you a good way to begin discussing the subject with your child.

Secrets

Children love secrets. Unfortunately some secrets, such as those about touching or kissing, just aren't safe. It is difficult to teach young children that there are 'good' secrets and 'bad' secrets. Some families get around this by using the term 'surprise secrets' for things like birthday presents or their Mummy having a baby. These 'surprise secrets' are always told, at some definite time. One mother I know doesn't use 'secrets' at all. She calls everything 'surprises' and says that all secrets are bad. The difficulty with this is that when children go to play group or to school, they soon learn that other children use the word 'secrets'. I would opt for 'surprise secrets', but you must choose what you feel your child understands best. The message to children is that secrets about presents or babies or moving house are OK, but secrets about touching, kissing or hugging are not.

You can tell your children that no one should ask them to keep any touching secret, and that they should tell you if someone does. They should tell *no matter what the person says, even if he or she threatens something bad will happen as a result.* Many young children have been afraid to tell because of threats made against them or their families. One four-year-old was abused by her babysitter, but didn't tell because the babysitter said the child's mother would die if she did.

In this story about touching, a babysitter is shown trying to get the child to play a 'secret game'. I have used a babysitter because of cases I have known in which young children have been abused while left in the care of a babysitter. However, you may choose to call the person a friend or uncle or some other name. Whatever you decide, the message about telling is the most important one you can teach your child.

At the end of each section, there are questions which will help reinforce the messages from the stories. Through the questions, the child can actively participate in learning with the help of the adult reading the story. The final question for each section suggests a way in which you can ask your children to share experiences, should you wish.

How much could a young child do if confronted with a dangerous situation? It is impossible to say, just as it is impossible to know if a child will put into practice the road safety rules we teach. However, one five-year-old recently saved a four-year-old from being abducted by a stranger because he had been taught to take care of himself (and others). Children cannot always be kept safe, but at least we can try to give them strategies for survival which may help.

Feeling Happy, Feeling Safe is comforting, colourful and fun. Yet it also teaches children to 'think safe'. It may be the most important book you ever read with them.

Michele Elliott

Meet the friends
in this book

Mike likes playing with his cat
and eating jelly.

Emma likes to swim
and go on picnics with
her family.

James likes to build
things and see
how they work.

Anne likes making plasticine models
and playing in the sand-pit
with her friends.

Feeling Safe

Mike and Emma were in the park. They raced to the slide and climbed the steps. Whoosh! Down they came. It was the best fun in the whole world.

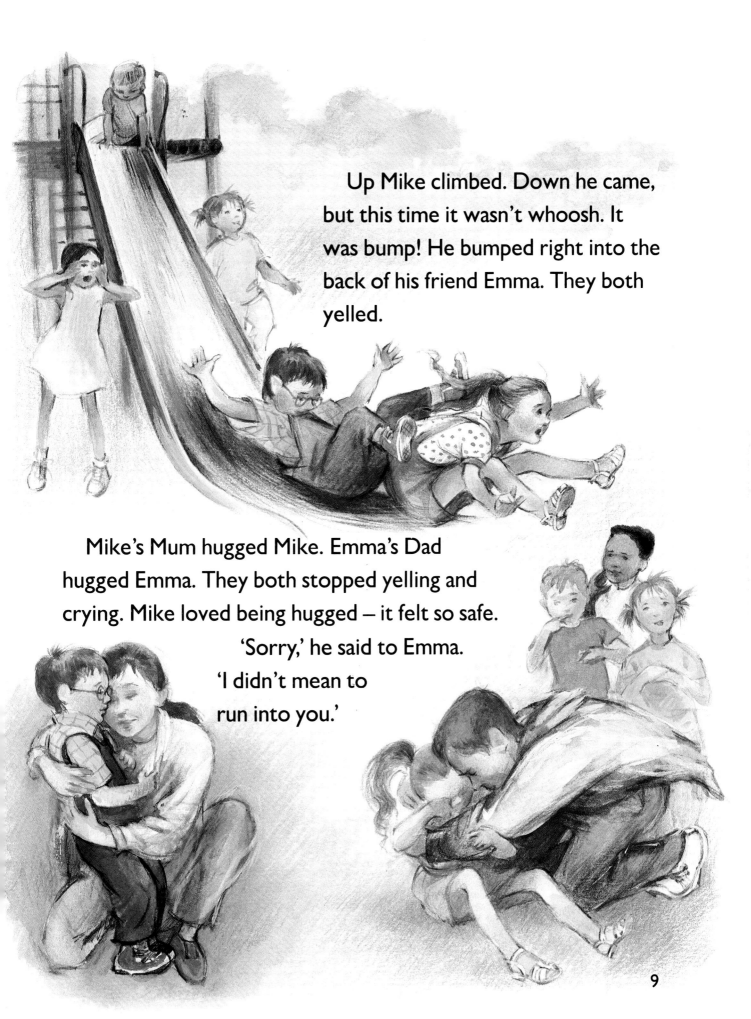

Up Mike climbed. Down he came, but this time it wasn't whoosh. It was bump! He bumped right into the back of his friend Emma. They both yelled.

Mike's Mum hugged Mike. Emma's Dad hugged Emma. They both stopped yelling and crying. Mike loved being hugged – it felt so safe.
'Sorry,' he said to Emma.
'I didn't mean to run into you.'

Mike and Emma felt happy and safe
again. Mike likes feeling safe. Emma
does, too.

What do you like to do that makes you feel happy?

When do you feel safe?

Who do you feel safe with?

Getting Lost

Anne and her Mum and Grandma were going shopping.

'Now remember, Anne,' said Mum, 'if you get lost, stay right where you saw me last and I'll come back for you. If you get scared, ask someone who works in the shop to help you. But don't go outside the shop.'

'OK, Mum,' said Anne.

Mum always said the same thing before they went shopping, but Anne had never got lost.

First they went to look at some towels and sheets.

'Boring,' thought Anne.

Then they went past the toys. Anne stopped

to look at a wonderful giant teddy. When she
turned round, Mum and Gran had gone. What
should she do? What had Mum told her? **She
must stay where she was if she ever got
lost.** So Anne sat down next to the giant teddy.
Mum and Gran would come back and find her.

Anne waited for a little while. It
seemed like a great long while to
her. It seemed like a whole year. She
knew she shouldn't go outside the
shop, so she waited and waited.

What else had Mum told her to do if she got lost? Anne tried
to remember. Oh, yes, she could ask someone who worked in the

shop to help her find Mum and Gran. But just as Anne got up to ask, Gran came round the corner.

'I thought you'd never find me,' cried Anne. 'I was really scared.'

'I know,' Gran said, 'but you're safe now. Look, here's Mum.'

Anne's Mum looked cross, but she picked up Anne and gave her a kiss.

'You frightened me, Anne-Marie.' She always called Anne, Anne-Marie, when she was cross. 'I shall turn you into a goose if you ever scare me like that again!'

Anne grinned. Mum always teased her about being a silly goose. It was nice to feel safe again.

What can you do if you feel unsafe?

Tell Gran

Tell Mum

Tell a police officer

What should you do if you ever get lost?

Stay where you are

Ask the shop lady

Wait patiently

Have you ever been lost?

Saying No

James, Anne, Mike and Emma and their friends all go to the same play group.

'What would you do if I said you had to eat that sand?' said Mrs Fowler one morning, pointing to the sandbox.

'Yuck,' shouted James, 'I wouldn't.'

'I'd tell my Mum,' said Anne.

'I'd say NO!' said Emma.

Mrs Fowler was smiling. 'Well done, all of you. You can say no if anyone asks you do something silly, or that would hurt you. Let's practise saying no. All together when I count three – 1, 2, 3...'

'No!' yelled Anne, Mike, James, Emma and the rest of the children.

'Louder,' said Mrs Fowler.

'NOOOOOOOO!' shouted the children.

'That's wonderful,' said Mrs Fowler. 'You're the champions!'

After play group, Anne went home with Emma to play.

'Stay in the garden,' said Emma's Mum. 'We're on a busy road, so don't go outside.'

Jenny, who lived next door, came to the gate.

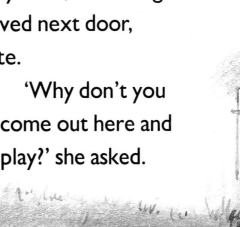

'Why don't you come out here and play?' she asked.

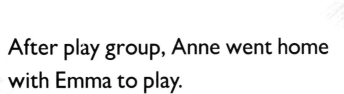

'Can't, Jenny. Mum said
not to,' replied Emma.
'Oh, come on.'
'No,' said Emma.
'You're silly. I bet Anne will come.'
'No thanks,' said Anne.
'Babies! Bet you two are just babies.'

Emma and Anne looked at
each other and then turned and
shouted NOOOOOOO in a
great loud voice.

Jenny went indoors and Emma's Mum came to
see what the fuss was about. When the girls told
her, she was very pleased they hadn't gone out
on to the busy road.

'Jenny was wrong to ask you to go
out,' she said. 'I'm glad you said no.
You're both big, sensible girls!'

When can you say no?

If something is dangerous

To a stranger in a car

To a bully

If you don't like something

Have you ever said no to anything?

When do you like to say yes?

Bullies

Mike was going to the park with his older cousins. His friends James, Emma and Anne were there, too, playing on the swings. Suddenly a bigger boy came over and started tugging the chains on Anne's swing. He tried to tip Anne off the swing. The swing began to sway from side to side. Anne was very frightened. Mike saw what was happening and ran to Anne.

'Come over here, quick,' he shouted to James and Emma.

James and Emma ran over, shouting as they came.

'Stop that!' yelled Emma.
'Leave her alone!' said James.
'I won't,' said the bully.
Then James opened his mouth and yelled NOOOO in the loudest voice Mike had ever heard. Anne and Emma joined in.

'NOOO!' they shouted. 'GO AWAY!'

The bully looked surprised. The big kids started running to help.

'NOOOO!' shouted the children again.

The big kids arrived just in time to see the bully running off. Mike's cousin laughed.

'You certainly know what to do if someone tries to hurt you,' he said. 'They could hear you shout all the way to the moon!'

What's a bully?

Someone who hurts you  Someone who hits you  Someone who's mean

What can we do about bullies?

Tell a grown-up  Get away  Shout No

Have you ever been bullied?

Someone You Don't Know

James knows that a stranger is someone you
don't know. All these people are strangers to
him. He knows he shouldn't talk to someone he
doesn't know if he isn't with Mum or Dad. Most
strangers are nice, but some are not. Some
strangers aren't safe; they may hurt a child. So
it's best not to talk to someone you don't know
if you're on your own.

Anne was playing in the sand-pit
when a stranger tried to talk to her.
She knew she shouldn't talk to
strangers when she was on her own,
so she pretended not to hear him.
Clever Anne!

'Mum,' Anne shouted, 'Mum,
please come here . . .' Mum came
straight away. 'I'm proud of you,
Anne,' she said. 'You knew just
what to do!'

Mike and his Mum know Mr
Shaw. He isn't a stranger. But
Mike still wouldn't go off with
him without telling his Mum or
Dad first.

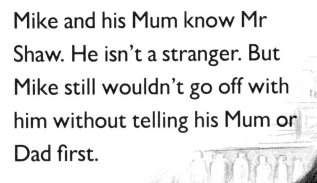

Emma and her Dad were buying ice-cream. It was hot! Emma said thank you to the ice-cream lady. The lady was a stranger but Emma wasn't on her own. Dad was with her. Emma wouldn't talk to the ice-cream lady if she were on her own, and she wouldn't go off with her.

If you ever got lost, a stranger might have to help you. Once James got lost in the street. His Mum had told him about asking the person in the shop. But James got lost outside! So he stayed right where he was, and didn't cross the road.

After a while, a man and a lady with a baby stopped to ask if he needed help. James nodded, but didn't get too close to them. He walked with them until they found a telephone box. He told them his name and his telephone number. They rang his Dad and he came to get him. Clever James knew his telephone number. Do you know yours?

What is a stranger?

What should you do if you are on your own and a stranger tries to grab you?

Shout for Mum

Run to whoever you're with

Run to a shop

What should you do if you are lost and have to talk to a stranger?

Don't hold hands

Don't get close

Tell a police officer

Touching

Mike, James, Emma and Anne were playing in the park, when a ladybird landed on Mike's arm.

'Look!' said Mike. 'The ladybird's walking on my arm. I like it. It's sort of tickly.'

'I don't,' said James. 'Don't like tickling.'

'My Mum says I don't have to be tickled,' said Anne.

'Why?' asked Emma.

'Because I don't like it, and it's my body,' said Anne. 'I can say no if I don't want my body tickled or touched.'

'But I like being tickled,' said Mike, 'on my toes.'

'Then you can say yes,' said Anne.

'I wish ladybirds gave hugs,' sighed James. 'I like hugs.'

'Me, too,' giggled Emma.

'But I don't like hard hugs. I can't breathe,' said Mike.

'I don't like hard smacks,' said James. 'Sometimes my brother hits me and it makes me cross.'

'Me, too,' said Emma and Anne together.

Anne laughed. 'Then we can say no.'

'And I can say yes to hugs!' shouted James. 'But where's the ladybird? She's gone.'

'She flew home to hug her children,' said Emma, 'but not too hard or she would have squashed them!'

What kind of touches do you like?

What kind of touches don't you like?

A hard tickle

Your hair pulled

Your face washed!

What can you do if you don't like a touch?

Say no

Tell a grown-up you know

27

Secrets

Some secrets are fun – like birthday presents.
Emma is longing to find out about the surprise
secrets in her presents.

Some things – like a hug – are never, ever
kept secret. Emma likes hugs from Gran and
Grandpa and from Mum and Dad and Uncle John.
Emma's family likes to hug and kiss. But they
don't keep kisses and hugs secret.

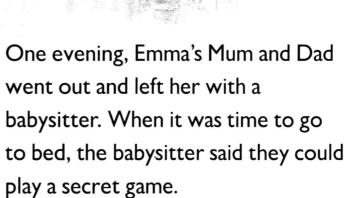

One evening, Emma's Mum and Dad went out and left her with a babysitter. When it was time to go to bed, the babysitter said they could play a secret game.

'What game?' asked Emma.

'You sit on my lap and I'll give you a kiss. The kiss is a special secret just between us,' said the babysitter. 'Then you can stay up late.'

Emma wanted to stay up late, but she didn't want to play the game.

'No,' said Emma. 'I don't want to.'

'You'd better,' said the babysitter, 'or your Mum will be angry. You'll be in trouble.'

But Emma didn't believe him. Her Mum had told her not to keep secrets. She knew her Mum wouldn't be cross.

'No,' she said again, 'I don't want to play.'

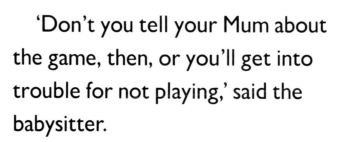

'Don't you tell your Mum about the game, then, or you'll get into trouble for not playing,' said the babysitter.

Emma didn't say anything. She nodded her head, but decided to tell her Mum and Dad the minute they came home. Emma lay in bed and listened for a long time until she heard her Mum and Dad come home. The babysitter left. Then Emma got out of bed and told them what had happened.

'I'm glad you told us, Emma. He shouldn't have asked you to keep a kiss secret,' said Dad.

'We never keep kisses or hugs secret,' said Mum.

Dad carried Emma back to bed and she snuggled down. Emma felt good, and soon fell fast asleep. She was safe and happy!

What should never, ever be kept secret?

What can you do if anyone ever asks you to keep a hug or kiss secret?

Say no

Who could you tell if someone asked you to keep kisses or hugs or touches secret?

Tell a grown-up you know

Dad   Mum   Grandpa   your aunt   your teacher   a police officer

What are some nice surprise secrets?

Kidscape Keepsafe Code

1 Hugs
Hugs and kisses are lovely. They should never be kept secret.

2 Body
Your body belongs to you.

3 No
It is OK to say no if someone tries to kiss or touch you and you don't want them to.

4 Run
If a stranger or bully tries to frighten you, run to your Mum or Dad or to a safe place.

5 Yell
It is OK to yell if you are scared and need help.

6 Tell
Tell a grown-up if you are frightened.

7 Secrets
Surprise secrets, such as birthday presents, are fun. But never ever keep kisses and hugs secret.

For a free colour-in poster of the **Kidscape Code**, or a copy of the free parents' guide and more information about KIDSCAPE, send a large self-addressed envelope to:

KIDSCAPE
World Trade Centre
Europe House
London E1 9AA
Telephone: 071-488 0488